Heal As You Reveal .....

A Follow up to the memoir *"I Was Somebody Before This"*

Dedicated to: Every victim/survivor of domestic and sexual abuse who's been silenced, victim shamed, or told they were lying.

~ The only people mad about you speaking the truth are the very ones busy living a lie~ unknown

Heal As You Reveal

Written and Published by : Kitti Jones

the publisher's authorization may be deemed illegal and punishable under the law.

Table Of Contents

Chapter One:
The Day My Life Changed

~Change is the law of life. And those who look only to the past or present are certain to miss the future~ JFK

I spent days reflecting that it had been several months since I had received that message in my inbox on social media. This photo was a young woman wearing the same clothes I was made to wear during my time with R. Kelly, the dreaded sweatpants and baggy top.

I was triggered by that photo. Before the woman sent me that photo, I had plans to ignore her. I wasn't going to help her because I'd never met her daughter or anyone new who had entered his life after I'd left in 2013. Once I saw the picture in sweats, there was no way I could live with myself not speaking to her at least once. I was able to share some very detailed things that could help validate some of this parents worse fears. Thinking that I was emotionally ok, I never saw this breakdown coming from just looking at a photo of someone I never met in sweatpants. My hurts were bottled up and put away never planning to revisit this period in my life ever again and I didn't know how this woman knew of me or who sent her. I didn't know the full reason she was frantic but felt like offering my help.

(August 2013,a month before leaving weighing 107 pounds)

She wasn't sure what her daughter was experiencing in the house with him (R. Kelly) and wanted to reach out after hearing rumors of inhumane treatment. I was pissed at what she was telling me, how could this man still be pulling these disgusting things with other women and girls? Feeling enraged, I shared with her that he was abusive towards me and had these strict rules, and used starvation as a way to punish me, which caused me to lose a massive amount of weight during my time with him.

I shared old photos and told her I'd be praying for her daughters safe return home and I went back under the radar. Still in complete shock I tried to enjoy NYE festivities in hopes to leave this behind me in 2016.

The top of 2017 had arrived and a Chicago reporter contacted me explaining his background. The reporter explained that he was familiar with me touring with R. Kelly, but was curious how I ended up with him and what happened during my time. We spoke for a couple of hours and I thought nothing more would come of it. If I remember correctly he explained that he may be doing an article or possibly something with a network, but he was having a hard time with them picking up the stories he'd put together for his expose'. When I heard this, I told him I wanted to stay anonymous. I was afraid of how people would treat me as I was working a regular job and now living a quiet life, minding my business. At that time in early 2017 R. Kelly was still booking shows and doing quite well. No one was writing about his private life or his past. Black women were still his main supporters and urban radio stations still praised him as King of R&B.

No scandals were out and very few people cared about his innocence or guilt from his 2008 acquittal. People who personally knew me noticed how my time with him had taken a toll on me, and they couldn't listen to his music anymore. Although I hadn't gone public yet,

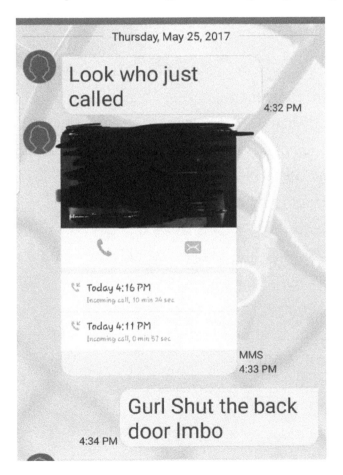

my close friends and family had a hunch, and never looked at him the same once I returned home. Was I ready for the world to know everything by talking to the Chicago reporter? The answer was No.

Out of nowhere one day in May 2017 calls from Rob came in, more than shocked, I was curious how he suddenly had my new number. How the hell did he get my number? I could never put my finger on it until months later. The phone call was definitely intimidating and I could tell he was trying to record me saying I had never been violated in any way by him, which he knew to be false. I would never fall for the trap, and only kept saying "Daddy where is all this coming from". I knew, that somehow he found out that I'd spoken to the reporter, or that parent, and maybe he started to panic.

In shock, I sent the screenshot of his calls to a friend, showing her the incoming calls from him. The very next day I saw a strange number come up and no voicemail, I googled it and it was the FBI. A source told me she had been contacted as well and that she'd spoken to them. I didn't have an attorney at that time and I didn't know what they wanted from me. I felt it was disrespectful to pass my number around with out asking me, so I changed it, and no one had it.

Months had gone by and I celebrated my birthday in July. I was living in Kansas and happy to be back around family and away from the vibes in Texas. I was still hurt, and being teased on radio by old colleagues when R. Kelly was in the news, although it had now been three years since I'd left Chicago. I was happy to be in another state, it was refreshing but I knew it wasn't my deep desire. I was very disappointed by old associates who treated me differently once I wasn't the "radio chick" anymore who could get them free tickets and VIP into clubs. I knew the day would soon come when I would no longer allow others to control how I operated, or play a part in me wanting to leave town.

I was busy trying to regain some normalcy and rebuild my life. Everyday task that most people would find to be simple, was agonizing for me the first couple years. Things as simple as going around crowds of people at grocery stores, or pumping gas. It took me a very long time to hold my head up and speak to random men. I would have anxiety and didn't know why I would be sitting in my car waiting for most of the cars to drive away at gas stations. I was nervous that the guys would try to talk to me, I was scared. I was indeed experiencing post-traumatic stress and had no idea. I had to keep reminding myself that nothing bad would happen to me, to just get out of the damn car. I would call someone on my cellphone to talk to me while I walked into stores so I could avoid communicating with people.

With Rob, I was prohibited from looking men in the eye, my head had to be down, facing him, or a wall. It was so embarrassing to have to do this when we were on tour because people who performed before us would try say hello to me and I came off rude not acknowledging them.

So here it is, July 17th 2017 and I wake up to a phone call telling me my name is being mentioned in the blogs regarding R. Kelly and a cult. I froze .... My name is in what? I replied in disbelief. I was barely awake and thought this chick was toying with me.I know this has to be a mistake! I had spoken to the Chicago reporter six months prior and thought since we never spoke again that this story he was working on had been canceled. Out of nowhere this story hit and it hit hard, everyone was talking about it.

"Well there goes my normal life and privacy in Kansas I'm fucked"!!! I thought. I logged in online and found the article and there it was, my name in full *"Kitti*

Jones claims ....". It was about Rob allegedly running a cult and holding women against their will. I wasn't ready for this, not now, please God. But if it were up to me I would have never been ready to discuss all the things that occurred during my time with Rob.

This was shocking for me to wake up to. I knew it was definitely time to stop running from this. It was time to make him uncomfortable with doing this to other women and young girls. In the past, he allegedly paid for silence of almost everyone who threatened to come forward. I was getting request to comment on the article and I got scared to give my name. I didn't know where to start, so I went anonymously on the radio and allowed them an interview, it was the first time. I realized that people were open to listening and not judging or shaming me. Many people in the radio business knew it was me by the description, so there was no hiding.

I didn't know it at that moment but my life was about to change and I was in for a long journey, one that would be inspiring for millions, and one that would have me paranoid and questioning many around me. The fighter in me didn't want to feel powerless ever again. There were women thanking me for standing up against such a megastar and if I could do it they could do it. I had to keep going, this was bigger than me.

Chapter Two:
The Naughty Reporter

~Nothing unmasks a man like his abuse of power~E.H

After that first public interview on the radio I was naïve to believe that it would end all the curiosity of the public. I received a request to fly out to another city to give my story to a popular news show. I figured "no sweat" this show isn't too bad, and hopeful that they would handle my story with delicacy. They were known for reporting headline news stories that were serious. I trusted them to help me bring awareness to what was happening behind closed doors during my time with Rob, and that it was still possibly happening according to others who had gone on record.

I took the flight and they interviewed me a few hours after I had arrived. I sat in their studio for 3-4 hours purging everything, crying when remembering all the things I had suppressed for 3 years. It was therapeutic for me, yet frightening. In one segment, the reporter had a pair of sweat pants, (he had the wardrobe lady go out and purchase) so that I could give an example of the clothes Rob required me to wear. He actually expected me to change into the sweatpants for the next shot and improvise. I was highly offended by this and declined. I offered to instead hold up the sweatpants and acknowledged that they were similar to what I had to wear. Wow! I thought this is so insensitive what the....? But that was only the beginning.

They took what they call pick up photos and shots of
me walking outside overlooking the water, and the
reporter started constantly reminding me of how
beautiful and intelligent I was. I thanked him for
having me, with a nervous smile I pretended to be
okay. I wasn't okay I had just shared some pretty
fucked up things in front of a room full of strangers for
the first time (previously I was only on the phone with
reporter and on the radio show). Sexual things I hadn't
shared, physical abuse and much more, and I was
ready to go to my hotel and cry my eyes out. They
were thanking me for coming and praising me for my
bravery. As soon as I got to the hotel a producer called
and said they wanted me to hold my story and not give
it to anyone else before they did. They said the story
was so compelling that they wanted to use it for season
premiere week in September which was six weeks
away.I was okay with that, I guess, but it only
benefited them. I was worried that no one would care
in six weeks and the story was serious and could help

other victims. They were in it for ratings this was not about helping black girls.

I agreed and signed a form after some convincing of how things work with fact checking my story and how long it could take but I still thought "Ugh what did I get myself into, I wondered". Later in the night a text came through from the reporter thanking me, it was harmless (A photo shot of his text is shared in this chapter with shaded name of the show and reporter) . I flew home the next morning drained from all the crying I did the day before. The reporter started texting me again asking if he could see me. I replied " See me how"? He said" I think you're a beautiful person and you didn't deserve that and I'd like to fly you back out sometime, maybe dinner and shopping too". I couldn't believe what I was reading. I just said "Wow thanks, I don't know". I was being polite and the next text said "I mean, I'm not filthy rich I'm just an old married man looking to be your friend".

I read that last text in disbelief. I wanted to cuss and flip out but what about my story? They had my story for six weeks, so I didn't want to be rude and ruin things.

I hired an attorney a few days before I did this news show and I sent her all these text messages from this reporter. She was floored and asked me what did I want to do because this was disgusting! She also witnessed him commenting under my Instagram page about wanting to pay my rent, he posted jokingly, but she could see right through it. He continued asking me for pics and I would just say "go to my page I posted today". I did everything to blow him off and was too afraid to report him because I thought my fate, and how people would perceive my story rested in his hands. I invested hours in that room telling these strangers my business for free, I didn't know what to do.

It was hard holding back from cursing him out. He would send me photos of himself at work or home. He started telling me what he loved to do sexually. I made a huge mistake by sending him a "LOL" which opened the door for more. Eventually he started to realize that my text would only be asking about the air date of my segment, one day he said "Ok no more inside info until I get a photo" I replied " Really ? You don't care about my story getting out"? He then replied "Of course, but I don't want that to be the topic between us all the time". I then told him "Sorry, what I shared was a very dark time in my life, I know that the world will judge me, and I'm scared, I thought I could ask questions, sorry if you feel mislead by any of my communication".

He went silent on me via text, but he would still tell me how beautiful I was on social media. I just started updating my lawyer and family daily on what I assumed was the air date since this guy was playing games. I wasn't about to send him personal photos of me in exchange for information when my story will air, screw him.

I was in rush hour traffic when calls started coming in telling me I was on TV and how it lasted all of three minutes. I was pissed because this horny fucker could have given me the heads up on the air date so I could have seen it, or told my family. The second reason I was livid was the fact that it was three minutes of him narrating the wrong timeline over me and then chopping my story up so bad it made me look ridiculous (at least to me). That asshole! I waited six weeks only to feel I had been silenced and manipulated again. I was done with this shit! If I was going to talk again it had to be in my own words unedited and with a real professional. I couldn't help but think he did this to me on purpose because I didn't take him up on his offers. This coming forward thing was looking like a long uphill battle. I wasn't going to be strong enough for this fight even praying about it I felt sad inside. Should I just let this shit go and go back under the radar ? I was starting to realize why many abuse victim

stories never get reported or get swept under the rug.
The abuse of power is real and often times the accuser
looks like the liar and opportunist. I wanted to keep my
hands clean and my head held high. I had no plans to
report the man it was too much on my plate already
and my attorney left that decision up to me.

Chapter Three:
Rolling Stone

~Pain shapes a woman into a warrior~

I moved back to Dallas and wasn't settled into my new place, boxes we're still packed and my car had no room left in it. I was too overwhelmed moving by myself from one state to another, so I put the idea of interviewing with Rolling Stone off a week. My attorney had contacted me about them being interested in my story.

I was close to giving up until my attorney informed me that the head editor from Rolling Stone was interested in flying out to speak with me personally. She knew how uncomfortable I was from the last ordeal and made it a promise to be present at this interview, if I agreed to a sit down. I woke up the day of the interview scared. I didn't like feeling like a victim of anything, people take advantage of you during your vulnerability. Men, friends, and the media were all treating me like I was a doormat because of this victim label. I was tired of people thinking because I shared these dark moments with Rob, that I was somehow a person they could take advantage of as well on other levels.

In short, I wasn't trying to walk into the interview looking like I was this sad ass weak bitch! I got dressed, and had a friend accompany me, and my attorney was there waiting at the office we agreed to meet at. I walked into this office space ironically it was the building of a man I used to date before Rob, he had also been responsible for introducing me to my attorney. I was hoping he wasn't around, I didn't want him watching me potentially breaking down telling my story. Thank God he was missing in action and only his staff was present in escorting me to the interview room.

I hugged my attorney and suddenly this tall attractive white guy says "Hi I'm (name redacted) from Rolling Stone, very honored to meet you and thank you for trusting me to tell your story", I'm thinking this wasn't a bad start at all. It was comfortable immediately for me, my female attorney was present, and I was in the surroundings I was familiar with "I'm good, let's go" He pressed record and I started from beginning to end of how my life was before I met the man that changed me forever. I walked him through my personal home life as a divorced mother whose child was living in Italy at the time and how it was being a radio personality in Dallas. I explained, that like most women, when we have everything else working in our favor in life, we want love. I explained in graphic detail the sex demands, beatings, the female that tortured me, touring with Rob, and being apart of his cage skits and how I left the man I gave up everything for after 2.5 years.

I was not looking for anyone to feel sorry for me, that wasn't my point coming forward. I had gone long enough hearing rumors about me and people spreading lies about what really happened that ultimately brought me home. I explained how disgusted I was once I found out he had kept this sick behavior going after I'd left.

The most hurtful and disgusting part in coming forward was the way I was treated by black women who owned blogs and radio platforms with millions of followers, they were controlling my story and making it a joke. They would post excerpts of me to confuse people and passive aggressively alluded to me being after Robs money. I had no lawsuit against him or planned one, and the idea of a book hadn't happened yet.

I was genuinely coming forward to help shed light and take my story out of the lying gossiping mouths of people who had a vendetta against me. These mean spirited bloggers were trying to silence me by using their platforms with millions of followers to make me look stupid. The comment sections of these urban bloggers were even more ignorant, laughing at a quote the blog put up of me describing being kicked and slapped by Rob for confronting him about an alleged sex-tape. I was horrified that these grown ass women and young adults thought domestic violence was funny.

The bloggers didn't care to acknowledge that I was showing evidence and never posted it. These people were looking at me like I was in this conspiracy to take down their King of R&B and that I was being paid to do it. I was sick of this shit I was reading and lost my faith in the black community because of them victim shaming me.

I realized that bloggers are in business to make money with their angles of your story and very uncomfortable with you telling it yourself , they can't make money when you beat them at their own game. I took control of my own narrative and was ready to put a stop to people lying for good. This publication was helping me do just that.

I knew that what I had lived to tell was bigger than a fucking Instagram blog and their ignorant following attacking me and that's why I was sitting with Rolling Stone, a respectable publication and professional reporting.

Talking to Rolling Stone felt like a relief. I waited three weeks for them to complete their fact checking. They spoke to people in the business who was around during our tour and saw what Rob was doing to me, old colleagues, family members and friends.

In addition, I turned over flight info, pictures, videos, text, and more. They had to do this to protect themselves from lawsuit. You can't just print a story like mine without proof.

October 23, 2017 I woke up with my heart pounding. I read a text message from my lawyer telling me that my Rolling Stone article will publish online that afternoon, This is the most fear I'd felt so far. It was fear from being judged for the choices I made when I didn't love myself enough. The world (not just a small group of people) was about to read about graphic detail of my time with R.Kelly and it wasn't easy processing this. For years prior, I always felt someone could mention something shameful I did with Rob and I hated that someone out there had the power to potentially embarrass me. It felt good putting it all out there once and for all , I felt powerful. I suddenly held my head high and prayed, I exhaled.

Within hours I looked at twitter and I was trending :

Goth-all-year Morsch
@girlwparasol

couldn't even make it through the Kitti Jones Rolling Stone article b/c it got too real. That shit is abuse. That man is a monster.

10/23/17, 6:35 PM

Scarlette stands 👠 @sar... ·1h ∨
@rkelly only an insecure lil thug
would abuse women & use young
girls as their private sex toys.
You're a POS. #KittiJones has
SPOKEN #SMALL

💬 ↻ ♡1 ✉

sachar @sacharmathias · 1h ∨
Replying to @sacharmathias
I believe **Kitti Jones**

💬 ↻1 ♡2 ✉

TheMoffattsVEVO @white... ·1h ∨
don't read the **Kitti Jones** R. Kelly
piece fr today if you don't want to
be thoroughly horrified
fuck @pitchfork
fuck @Bonnaroo
fuck @ifc

Linda
@LuckyPenny60

I believed the story about his first victim years ago & have no problem believing Kitti Jones. R. Kelly should be in prison. #BelieveWomen

Janet Mock ✔ @janetmock
A tough yet necessary read. Kitti Jones, one of many black women abused by R. Kelly, shares her experience. rollingstone.com/culture/featur...

TheMoffattsVEVO
@whitesedan

don't read the Kitti Jones R. Kelly piece fr today if you don't want to be thoroughly horrified
fuck @pitchfork
fuck @Bonnaroo
fuck @ifc

10/23/17, 7:08 PM

The day had come when I had gotten my voice back !! The day had come that I was supported! The name of my Rolling Stone article was "SURVIVING R.KELLY" (the title was later used for the now award winning Lifetime documentary)

Prayer:

"Thank you God, I will walk this journey in truth and try my best to help anyone who needs it, cover me and protect me as I will face obstacles and evil coming my way from people who won't agree with my path and hate me for speaking out! Protect my family from the backlash, they are innocent. Keep me strong, Amen!"

Chapter Four:
Book and Film Offer

~You either walk inside your story and own it, or stand outside of it and hustle for your worthiness ~

My article had gone viral and this had mainstream media hunting me down for more. Wendy Williams had a segment on her show repeating things I had shared with Rolling Stone. Wendy wasn't mean or shaming me, but she appeared to be on the fence and invited me to visit her show. I was contacted by her producer inviting me to the show and I never decided on it. For me, again, it wasn't about convincing people, no victim of any type of abuse should constantly have to defend themselves publicly. By telling my story some felt I was obligated to convince them to like me or believe me. I truly didn't give a fuck about being liked, my main concern was exposing the abuse, controlling my narrative, and providing my evidence. I didn't owe anyone shit and I wanted people to stop treating me like I did, EVERYONE!

My family and real friends were very supportive. Strangely people can get very comfortable with you being vulnerable and uncertain, but the moment the new you starts to emerge, they can't adjust. I wasn't down for anyone trying to make me feel bad for regaining my self-confidence and my life back. People that I thought I could trust were sending me all these bad screenshots of Facebook accounts making up lies about me, and calling me hoes for being with Robert. After four years of living with that shame, some didn't like that I was empowering myself. I guess there's satisfaction with me having my head down and living under the radar. I quickly changed my number again and stopped communicating with people who seemed to get hard-ons from me being upset over ignorance.

Sway Calloway Show was the only urban outlet at the time that I'd agreed to speak with, (after the article was released that week) he had a huge platform, and his approach was respectful. After all the attention, my former radio station decided to contact me and capitalize. Yes, the same station that radio personalities embarrassed me for years after I'd quit working for them, teasing me over dating R. Kelly. They said they wanted an interview and to offer an apology. After conversing with the GM for an hour, I agreed. They publicly apologized and I put it behind me. I couldn't help but wonder after I had outed the way they treated me in my article with Rolling Stone if it made them believe I was potentially thinking of a lawsuit. Whatever the case, I didn't like some people who still worked there, and I wanted to hurry and get the fuck out of the building after the interview.

I was drained I didn't want to keep talking about this but I knew I was helping women and girls across the world that read my article. I started getting inbox messages and emails from people thanking me and telling me they cried reading my story. Each time I didn't want to continue speaking out I'd see a reason to keep going.

One night after turning down interview after interview I said to myself, what if I write a book? I can just fill in all the holes and answer every question on everyone's mind about where I am now, and what happened. I began pondering this idea of a memoir. I pulled out my raggedy laptop and started typing away I asked another girl who had experience about book covers and self publishing, she told me what tools to use online. I googled and found all that I needed and created " *I Was Somebody Before This*" a 14 chapter book unedited and raw. The cover included a makeup free photo of me. I wanted the world to see that I wasn't hiding and I don't have a reason anymore. Take me as I am! This is me!

Within six days I was finished writing the memoir and released the chapters on my Instagram page. Before I knew it BET, Essence, and other media outlets were reporting that I had written a tell-all making it sound like a scandalous book of me outing people and it wasn't that at all. I was pissed, but people close to me told me to look at the bright side, this was free book promo, and advised that since people are watching my every move use it to my advantage. I couldn't argue with free promo but I certainly hated the narrative they were putting out about my book before even reading the mother fucker. Ugh!

The purpose of the memoir was to forever have my entire story for people to access, so I didn't have to keep repeating things over and over, not just surrounding who I dated but where I came from, my career and my dreams, and how I got to that dark place all in one book so there are no questions ever again.

Dating R. Kelly was a defining moment in my life and I wanted people to know that it didn't define me. But before I got to that freeing place I yearned to be in, I needed to air all this out and be courageous in the process.

I released the memoir on November 15th. I self published with no editor other than my attorney looking over the manuscript to make sure I disguised names and situations slightly enough to prevent lawsuits. My sales were through the roof! I was overwhelmed. I was feeling proud of myself and all I had done the last three months. The good and the bad and the uncertainty all came down to this moment. I was a new author and I embraced it!

The holidays were about to roll in, we were a week away from Thanksgiving. I went driving early morning to grab breakfast and I noticed an email alert from someone and the subject read ; Life and Book Rights. I didn't know what the hell that meant, so I tapped in while traffic had slowed and saw it was someone claiming to be from Lifetime network interested in paying me for my rights. I didn't understand until I kept reading, and it said they wanted to turn my book into a movie on their channel and made me a large offer to do so.

This is not real, I thought. Let me pull over and read this again. Here I was with one hell of a year, ending it back in Texas and telling my story to the world, and writing a book with no help, and now Lifetime wanted it? I put my hand over my mouth containing my screams and sobbed. I'm on the freaking service road looking crazy!

I frantically tried to snap out of crying and called my attorney to share the news. I began thinking someone was playing with me and I got scared. My lawyer would not pick up after the second attempt. I then googled the person who sent the email and saw that it was a legit offer and the email was real. My lawyer sent me a text asking if I was okay, and informed me that she would call after she left a meeting. I waited and shared the news with her and she was calm and collected. I was a little annoyed that I had gotten so excited and anxious only to hear her not sound very impressed. She had experience dealing with networks in her field and she didn't believe anything until it was in writing, she lived by it. I had to remind myself not to take her reaction personal and that she had my best interest. The following Monday the contract was in my email and after agreeing to terms I sold my rights (aka optioned). Who knew it would end this way? Not me! I had to keep this under wraps until they were ready to announce it to the world. I only shared this news with close friends and family at the time (later announced the film news in May 2018 on Megyn Kelly Show on NBC).

After I signed the contract this popular production
company contacted me, that claimed they were putting
together a documentary based on the article that had
come out regarding women who had lived with R.
Kelly, and parents who wanted their daughters out of
his home. They knew about me from Rolling Stone but
no one knew about my Lifetime deal because hadn't
been announced and I wasn't allowed to tell. After
going back and forth I signed on to see if this would be
something that would be impactful. At this time myself
and two other women were the only ones known to
have come out that year and we were the only ones
outside a set of parents being considered for the
documentary.

I didn't think much of it at first, I felt that each person
involved had stories that were compelling, and hoped

it could inspire and help abuse victims across the world .

Chapter Five:
Downside and Therapy

~The wicked will defend wicked~

After processing everything over the thanksgiving holiday, things I would read online would say; Why Kitti Jones ? Why is she being supported, she wasn't underage dealing with R.Kelly! Many people who hated the attention I was getting screamed this from the rooftops as much as possible. I was offended that certain people involved with this story wanted to silence me, I didn't understand. I realized that people were used to just hearing about underage allegations concerning R.Kelly. The truth is, he dated plenty of grown women and during my time with him I never witnessed anyone underage, but no one liked harping on that. Despite how many disturbing things I shared publicly, to some, only exposing his alleged attraction to teenage girls was all they wanted highlighted. It was definitely important that pedophilia was exposed, but what I shared was exposing another layer to the man they only heard one side of. I was done trying to defend myself against ignorance. I knew then that I couldn't rely on anyone but my family and the few outside of it for support.

It was not fair, but I started to see again, that this was going to be a battle I didn't feel like fighting. I had been through enough shit, and despised people who were quick to offend me by something they assumed and didn't know what they were talking about. I asked a woman privately; Why are you so pissed at me for telling the public about my time with R.Kelly? She said " I just don't believe you" I said " What part of my story don't you believe?" She then replied " I don't know it just seems fishy that you waited 3/4 years, seems money driven". It was then that I realized many people who were attacking me never read my

story, they just saw "Former DJ tells story of abuse"
and they formed a quick assumption. I was disgusted
with some of the backlash. Regardless of opinion, I
didn't deserve those beatings and torture even if I had
decided to sue him or make money for talking about it.
Who the fuck did these people think they were? The
word victim always made me cringe because I hated
feeling powerless all over again. I realized, I was the
closest these trolling assholes would ever get to the
man they admired and defended ,so after a few tweets
of me lashing out, I gave up on them.

Mainstream press took my story seriously, not only
because I had evidence, but because the climate was
changing in Hollywood and the industry. The week my

article released was the same week the "Me Too" Movement hashtag was strong exposing a lot of powerful men in the industry. The timing of my story played a huge part. So many women in Hollywood began coming forward about Harvey Weinstein and he started losing position in places and people were believing and supporting the women who came forward against him with respect.

I watched black owned publications and urban bloggers praise these women who were mostly white and support them. They were being talked about differently and not painted as groupies, gold diggers, liars, or hoes who wanted it, they were heroic. They graced the cover of Time Magazine for being brave. I wasn't an actress but I was a woman who had a good life and career when I met Rob, and again what happened to me was not deserving, regardless of my economic or social status. It was like, they were punishing me for exposing R.Kelly in my own community. It was exhausting wondering why, but I

Kitti Jones 🏆
@ikittijones

Never tell your serious story to trash blogs who have despicable followings, it will be made into a mockery for them to bash u! Preserve ☝️

12:54 PM · 9/28/17 · Twitter Web App

knew the truth deep down. I had a right to be heard. They had me fucked up, and it just made me go harder.

My book was a hit, but things started to get real. I didn't have a personal life anymore my days were being consumed with people constantly talking to me about R. Kelly. Old friends and people from my past that I hadn't spoken to in years would reach out, pretend it was just a "hello" but the conversation would shift to something they read or saw online about him. I felt people were baiting me into learning my thoughts of everything they read on blogs about me or him or other women who came forward. I wished there was an off button for most of my day. I did block and filter my social media so I wouldn't constantly see his name from reposted articles.

It's now early December 2017 and I'm in the news again because Rob was now in Dallas in concert and people were hitting me up for my reaction. I turned down request for a lot of local interviews but I did speak with a news station via phone giving my thoughts on the movement to shut down his concert that night. I thought since this is where I live, that maybe at least my old station would stop playing his music (after acting like they supported me when I sat with them to interview last month) but they didn't in fact both of their stations were actively playing him.

There was another local morning show ran by a black female, who had the audacity to put R.Kelly on their morning via phone, and support his show that night. I was floored because this same woman that I'd listened to over the years was outspoken about her mother being abused and her seeing it happen as a child. Very similar to my back story. To top it off, she's advocate during domestic violence month. Here this woman is giggling and laughing and co-signing Rob. I had no support in my city this was fucking tragic! I didn't know if it was revenge for me declining to interview previously or just ignorance! Fuck them!

The concert wasn't shut down, but the show in Oklahoma the next day was, they'd gotten wind of the uproar. Trolls started flooding my inbox and I noticed quickly by what one of the trolls was saying that it was someone that was close to the R.Kelly saga . I reached out to the person I felt it could be pretending I didn't

know this bitch was into terrorizing me online out of
pure hate and jealousy. I later hired a detective who
was able to help me pinpoint where the troll location
was and boom! I had the power in my hands, and
waited for the right moment to expose what I knew
(months down the line) .

This is the drama and downside to coming forward.
Unfortunately, because of the man being famous,
black, and wealthy many in the black community was
side eyeing me. In the black community we deal with
enough racism and false accusations and racial
profiling by law enforcement, so when another black
person destroys someone they feel has beat the odds,
they look for the flaw in the accusers to deflect
everyone from the truth.

My story was destroying the wedding songs, backyard
bbq, memories, and graduation songs fans used by
R.Kelly. During this time again it dawned on me how

all my hurts during this journey continued to be from black women, it made me depressed. I started feeling paranoid about people and their motives and I went off social media for a while. Around Christmas, I went back onto twitter out of boredom, and noticed I was being thanked in New York Times for coming forward along with Harvey Weinstein survivors written by Jennifer W. titled "Women to be Thankful For". I couldn't believe my eyes, it was confirmation to not get down on myself no matter what, because there were people out there that recognized and appreciated my journey. Still something felt dark when I would get online and it was weighing on me heavily. I didn't like giving people access into my life anymore. I'd shared more than enough. I was careful about posting my location as well.

Inside, a part of me felt sorry for Rob. I wasn't doing this to make him lose everything like people thought. I just wanted him to stop hurting others, and to get some professional help. I wanted to take my power back

from gossipers and the man who once broke me down.
I was searching for a peace of mind now, but I felt
people wouldn't let me have it.

I had everything to be happy about. My finances are
great, the book is a hit, and I have this movie about my
life with Lifetime, and now a documentary I'd just
signed on to do with this production company. I didn't
know yet that the documentary would end up on
Lifetime, the same network who had my movie. Once I
found out it made sense to do the documentary as long
as entities stayed separate.

Dealing with so much in so little time was
overwhelming, and I didn't want to become depressed.
I may have been already depressed, but I wasn't
owning up to it. I found a therapist and I immediately
felt comfortable with her. I would go every Tuesday
and Thursday in the beginning and then once a week. I

could vent all my frustrations and she would reel me back in with a reason to love myself even more. I was sold on her. I expressed my fears of dating again and how I sabotage things when guys seem to get to clingy or want sexual contact too much. I was late in realizing I had these post traumatic experiences. It felt good putting things into perspective and not thinking I was nuts . I was able to pinpoint my hurts and disappointments. She helped me understand why I wanted acceptance from other black women after I explained my hurts by black media. Without getting into the exact reason, her answers connected and resonated with me deeply. Now, I no longer put much stock into them rejecting me. Often times these people are projecting things onto you that they have yet to confront in themselves. Many suppress shameful things and ridicule others that are being courageous and brave, meanwhile they are still living a lie or hiding. Time and time again, I see women online laughing or blaming other women for being dumped, disrespected, abused, or cheated on. Several urban

female bloggers have made a living off posting stories
of men cheating or abusing black women. When they
post about the cheating, it's not set up to sympathize,
it's to further embarrass, and they leave the ignorant
comment sections to do the rest of the dirty work. The
comments are foul and disgusting of other black
women calling the woman hoes, and saying that's what
she deserved for dating him. They make fun of looks,
they bash the women for not being attractive enough
and more reasons blame her for his indiscretions. This
bullying also happened to me, and it caused me more
depression. Not only are you standing up against your
ex, his trolls, and non believers, you now have women
who don't even give a damn about your story, they just
want to bring you down because it's thrilling for them.
Many of those women were projecting there own
undesirable feelings about themselves onto me.

I felt so much better putting these things into
perspective in therapy. I did have plenty of reasons to

be proud of myself, and I wasn't about to let anyone ruin it. I was ready to start getting back out of the house and out of this funk. Therapy did me justice, it better had, that shit wasn't cheap, I thought. I stopped attending therapy mid February 2018 I never went on any medication or needed it. I do not suggest anyone take the path I did, I'm not advocating either way when it comes to meds. The therapy and constant prayer and focus helped me survive the downside to coming forward.

Anyone dealing with depression please notice the signs and reach out to someone professional for help . I didn't know I was depressed or dealing with post traumatic stress until I compared warning signs to my symptoms online. Don't be afraid to get help. The longer you wait the worse it can and will become . Depression can spill over into your personal relationships with others and how you react to things in general. There are so many resources and hotlines available for help.

SEXUAL VIOLENCE, ASSAULT AND CRISIS RESOURCES
National Domestic Violence Hotline
Crisis Text Line offers free 24/7 confidential crisis support for
people anywhere in the US to text with a trained crisis counselor.
Text HOME to 741741 to be connected to a trained crisis counselor
    Highly-trained advocates are available 24/7/365 to talk
confidentially with anyone experiencing
 domestic violence, seeking resources or information, or
questioning unhealthy aspects of their
 relationship.
Chat: http://www.thehotline.org/

Chapter Six:
Friends, Dating & Foes

Foe;

a person who feels enmity, hatred, or malice toward another; enemy:

a bitter foe.

Friend:

a person whom one knows and with whom one has a bond of mutual affection

I have always been open to befriending people from all walks of life. Each of my friends, add a different value to the friendship. I cherish my time invested in people and when things soured it would cut me deeply. I wondered why they didn't care like I did. I had to start operating on what provided me a peace of mind, and not expect anyone to have the same heart as me, I felt this approach, would save me from being let down anymore. Having expectations is not a lot to ask, or is it? Mutual respect and loyalty is number one, no exceptions.

During this period after being in the media for the last 8 months, there was a drastic change with a few friendships that I thought were solid. My therapist pointed out, that the things I began noticing, were already present, and basically when you walk into your light, you see everything clearer. Was I just dumb for not recognizing that people actually didn't have the same respect for me as I did them? No, life is all about lessons and offering your wisdom to the next person. Unfortunately, a very close friend and I had started becoming distant. I was not the same person, I had blossomed into my journey and the new improved version of me had emerged. Maybe this new me was uncomfortable for some. Were they really happy for me, at least they said it verbally, but actions were different. This friend began leaving me out of girls nights or outings, and would replace me with other people she knew, this hurt my feelings because I never knew anything was wrong. She would agree to something with me, and I would be waiting for her call to meet up, and I'd log into social media to see photos

that she'd be with someone else instead, doing what
we planned. I got tired of being treated this way and
not confronting people about how they made me feel. I
just went cold and avoided her and haven't seen or
spoken to her since.

" People come into your path for a reason, a season or
a lifetime:

*When you know which one it is, you will know
what to do with that person.*
*When someone is in your life for a REASON it is
usually to meet a need you have expressed.*
*They have come to assist you through a
difficulty...*
To provide you with guidance and support...
To aid you physically, emotionally or spiritually...
*They may seem like they are a godsend, and they
are.*
*They are there for the reason you need them to
be.*

Then without any wrongdoing on your part, or at an inconvenient time, this person will say or do something to bring the relationship to an end.
Sometimes they die...
Sometimes they walk away...
Sometimes they act up and force you to take a stand....
What we must realize is that our need has been met, our desire fulfilled...
Their work is done.
The prayer you sent up has now been answered and now it is time to move on.
Some people come into your life for a SEASON. Because your turn has come to share, grow or learn.
They bring you an experience of peace or make you laugh.
They may teach you something you have never done.
They usually give you an unbelievable amount of joy.
Believe it, it is real. But only for a season.
LIFETIME relationships teach you lifetime lessons.
Things you must build upon to have a solid emotional foundation.

Your job is to accept the lesson, love the person, and put what you have learned to use in all other relationships and areas of your life.
It is said that love is blind, but friendship is clairvoyant.
Thank you for being a part of my life...
Whether you were a reason, a season or a lifetime"

—Unknown

I wrote a letter to myself in therapy as a reminder that I was on the right path, and that I wasn't being inconsiderate to others, despite the new me that was emerging. I began accepting people for who they were. I approached every single thing in my life moving forward, differently.

The most disappointing was watching a few people publicly happy to say they were my friend, tag me online in things for the attention, and praise me for my bravery, but in private I wouldn't hear from them. Some wouldn't reach out unless my name was in a blog or news just to get a live reaction. I wanted to cuss them all out but therapy was the reason I stopped giving a fuck about things I couldn't control. The only person responsible for my happiness was me. Letting go of people who did questionable things was freeing. I could no longer afford to have those kind of people in my life. I sent confidentially agreements to everyone who was close to me, everyone signed with no problem, and nothing to hide, except two. I had to move different. In my journey, I was clean, no one was able to discredit me or pull up something crazy from my past to deflect people from what Rob did to me. I had to protect myself, this was serious.

Not every friend turned out to be a foe. A couple of childhood friends stepped up and showed no signs of being uncomfortable with me finding myself again. One friend showed her realness, it took us many months to get to a trusting place after an old betrayal, a friend since we were nine years old. The longest and most sincere friend I have currently. My other friendships seemed sincere, they would not mention anything in the press to me, and would invite me to paint parties and birthday events. Not all was bad, I didn't know why some friendships were being exposed as fakes but I wasn't upset about it anymore. The timing was great actually. When entering another level in your life the things that aren't meant to go with you will be exposed and fall off, I loved these epiphanies.

Months prior to this, I noticed a troll who would mention my son a lot and I hadn't publicly talked about him at all. I only defended not leaving him to be with R.Kelly like blogs made it sound. It was a narrative created to make me look like a bad mom so I wouldn't get support. This troll basically acted like I deserved to be beaten and starved. My son was living in Milan, Italy during my time with Rob. I hated these bitches playing with me about my child, any mother would.

This person was lying, and tagging blogs to cause controversy. I decided to hire a detective to find out who this person was invested in attacking me. Low and behold she was right under my nose. A friend from the past that had I recently reached out to, suspicious that she was behind this.

 Although we hadn't been close for years, I thought this person had enough class to not troll me online, and insult me as a mother. Was she jealous of the support I was getting? This wasn't a glamorous thing or something anyone should envy, so what the hell was the issue? She hadn't done this in the past, so why now? As I mentioned before, many became uncomfortable with me for speaking out. My ex husband once told me that he could see this jealousy in her towards me, and I would never acknowledge it. It is always the people around you, who love you, that notice these things before you do.

I thought, what a sick bitch! I wanted revenge for her lying about my child. Ironically, this person was living a nightmare in her own personal life with cheating and a bad marriage. She was miserable in her personal life and I guess trolling me fulfilled something.

After it was all confirmed to be her, I didn't feel the need to confront her, her life was messy already, and karma was probably paying her a visit without me getting my hands dirty. She disappeared on her own, good riddance.

I knew that I was being watched heavily online. My every move was under a microscope by non-supporters to catch me in a lie, or doing something that would discredit me. The last thing I wanted to do was give anyone a reason to make me out to be crazy by arguing with an anonymous account online. I had outed some of the troll names in Spin Magazine summer 2018. They highlighted the ups and downs of coming forward and what my life had been like. I had gotten the last laugh more than once. When you choose to forgive those that have hurt you , you take away their power.

As for dating, I have plans to love again one day. For now, it's a beautiful thing developing friendships and taking the time I need to be the best me before I decide on love again. I haven't given a lot of time to dating because of lack of interest in anyone. My priority is to thrive in other areas that I enjoy like writing and traveling. I don't believe in the term "follow your heart" anymore, our hearts can be persuaded by deception. Everything I do is based on my instincts, along with prayer, and common sense.

In the end, I have healthy friendships now. Having solid support is essential in your healing process. I'm grateful for friends and close family members.

My advice to anyone planning to come forward, make sure that your support system is solid and full of genuine people who love you unconditionally. Your support system should uplift you, keep you sane, and root for you becoming a better version of yourself. These will be the people that can detect when you are not ok, just by hearing your voice on the phone, and show up at your house to make sure nothing is wrong. More friends than foes. 🩶

Heal As You Reveal

Chapter Seven:
Filming Surviving R.Kelly

~Remember how many people would like to see you lose, it is your duty to make them wait forever ~

It hadn't been publicly announced that a documentary was in the works, but I was told that Rob somehow found out that this was potentially happening. I always felt there were people attaching themselves to other victims and getting information to take back to him. Later this was found to be true. I was just glad that I was on top of things, and remembered how he operated. Rumors started flying that he'd hooked up with Wendy Williams after hearing Lifetimes plan, and did a sit down interview with her (which she later admitted to but never aired it). He was desperate to shut us all up and paint us as liars. By this time, it seemed to be four more girls that had come out after me. I didn't know anything about them, but hoped they were finding some closure in their decision to come forward.

"Hi is this Kitti Jones"? said a male voice on the other end of my phone, it was a producer on the line explaining that he was ready to introduce me to someone, a woman that would be apart of running the documentary. I was given the dates of shooting this documentary that had been in the works for four months. Taping was set for March 2018, and I was being told I would be flying out later in that month to LA for my sit down interview on camera.

Life was good for me, I had my therapy, and my personal life was in order. Around this time, I was getting all these amazing updates about the movie based on my book with Lifetime, they were still developing the script, and combing through all the particulars. I was happier than I had been in years. Life was treating me well.

After the phone call, I started to think of all the hell I had been through with black media and bloggers. I wasn't sure how I would take to this black woman interviewing me on the doc about R.Kelly. I thought , oh shit, this is going to be me on defense the whole time, and I'm probably going to lose my composure.

During the month of March I started binge eating a lot and agonizing over this documentary. I wasn't sure if this was exploitation or what. How would this help the victims? I didn't know, but I put things into perspective by realizing that they were putting themselves on the line doing something that had never been done before. They were providing a platform for black women to come together, and share detailed accounts of their abuse. A few networks that were black owned or operated snubbed myself and others and wouldn't dare touch our stories. I spoke with a producer from a popular network owned by a "major force", just months prior, and later found out they allegedly didn't want to touch anything related to R.Kelly or his victims (Later this same "force" was open to interviewing white men accusing another mega star of abuse). Again, I felt we were being treated like we were trash in the black community by those that had the power to help. I felt somewhat grateful for Lifetime at this point.

I landed in Burbank and took a car to my hotel, and we were scheduled to film the next afternoon. I was fine until I began receiving text from the documentary staff providing wardrobe requirements and advised me to show up makeup free. It wasn't about the request itself, it was starting to dawn on me that I was about to appear on camera with god knows how many other people reliving things again. I didn't have an issue summarizing, letting people know what life was for me today, how I had gotten therapy, and how I released a successful memoir "*I Was Somebody Before This*". I hated when people thought it was easy to walk through moments of torture for their personal thrills or whatever they got out of it, I was hoping that this was not going to be a shit show. I hadn't met any of R.Kellys other victims that had come forward, except one, months prior.

It was explained to me that I wouldn't be sharing a camera with others, it would be just me. I felt so relieved, I wasn't comfortable hearing anyone else's story about him. I never wanted to read anything about him after I came out. I wanted to believe that others saw me be embraced by mainstream media, and be brave enough to write a book, that it inspired them to come forward as well. I just wanted to get it over with.

I didn't sleep well the night before taping. I woke up praying and I wanted to back out but it was too late. I had signed a contract and was paid for my materials for them to use.

Materials are your personal evidence that you allow them access to so they can fact check your claims, for example , videos , screenshots , witnesses , text , emails , flight information and more. They cannot and will not pay anyone to tell their story, it's bribery if so. Many people thought there was money being made in coming forward, or doing interviews, and it was such a lie. I hated reading comments from people assuming myself and others were making money from interviews, I hated the ignorance.

The staff personally made me feel comfortable as soon as I arrived to the studio. I met with everyone as I was in the makeup chair. I had shown up natural and very little on my lips and light powder on my face . The makeup girl had packed me down with a true beat (a term used for a full face of makeup). For this documentary, I didn't feel I should be glammed up like I was headed to a party. One of the people in charge of the show saw my makeup, and thought it was too much. Back in the chair I went, with almost the look I had when I walked in. After toning down my makeup I decided on what to wear with the staff and they put a mic on me. I sat in this chair and immediately I felt myself shaking so I crossed my legs so it wouldn't look obvious that my legs were moving on camera. Yikes, there were at least 10 people including camera men in this area and these bright lights were hitting my face. They were all setting up and preparing for action. I felt guarded because I couldn't help but remember how a lot of black women had treated me in this journey, and now a black woman was asking me questions on camera for this documentary. I wasn't looking for a fight but I was ready to go hard if I oven.

14h   450 likes   Reply

—— View replies (77)

These comments are proof you guys are dumb as hell

14h   489 likes   Reply

—— View replies (19)

Here she is fine for black women and in the comments black Women making fun of her, amazing!

13h   378 likes   Reply

—— View replies (18)

Bill Cosby ain't slick 😂😂

14h   347 likes   Reply

—— View replies (49)

She Look Like Lira Galore Babydaddy

14h   378 likes   Reply

—— View replies (92)

Y'all want me to believe rkelly hog tied this 😂😂😂😂😂😂

needed to. I sat up straight and looked confident. I had done my therapy and no one could break me down if they tried, I thought. As the questions began one by one I started losing this fake persona I was trying to put on for the camera, acting like I had it altogether.

I started to reveal in detail (much like I had done in my book) the first time Rob had disappointed me. I spoke about the night I moved to Chicago, waiting hours for him to arrive, I was pissed after I had given up so much to be there with him as we planned finally, I felt I deserved more respect. I walked them through how he beat me once I realized who the person was in the alleged sex-tape. I broke down in front of all those strangers and I was scared. Slowly my body wasn't sitting up so straight anymore. I wanted them to cut, and they did take a break, while I sobbed off camera, forgetting I was still with a microphone. I didn't know this at the time, but there was another set of staff members watching from a sound room, and I heard they were emotional too. I saw the black woman who was interviewing me in the hallway crying about the things I shared. When I saw her tears with my own eyes, I no longer had reservations about this projects motives, my guard was down. I sat in that chair for almost 10 hours off and on having to take breaks.

I allowed myself to cry openly without apologizing and feeling shame. I allowed myself to say "fuck him" for doing this to me! I owned up to not loving myself enough, which caused me to make bad decisions with men. Sure I cried during my Rolling Stone interview, and the news show prior to that, but it was different, I wasn't scared anymore or guarded. I was sharing my deepest feelings and dark moments, and it was helping my healing process while filming this documentary. Therapy had nothing on this shit, where the fuck was my refund, I thought. I walked out of there feeling like I could take on anything.

I knew after I was finished taping that something huge was emerging from this, and at the time I didn't know why I had this feeling. They hadn't named the documentary yet. The entire summer of 2018 they were taping and more and more people from Robs past were being added. I wasn't privy to knowing who else was included, but I knew it was taking long to be released for this reason.

September 2018 had come and I was asked to film a PSA for Lifetime for domestic violence month. I was honored to be chosen for this. I was taping this in New York and this is where I met the "Me Too" founder who was also apart of the PSA, along with Alyssa Milano, and Amanda Nguyen founder of Rise now. I was amongst some prominent women that I respected, and I was happy to be apart of the PSA. The PSA ran the entire month of October. I was so proud, and realized that exactly one year ago I was at the mercy of this shitty reporter hitting on me when I was just trying to share my story in the beginning, and here I am now with a national PSA with these women.

What a difference a year makes. A national PSA, I had completed my portion of filming the documentary, and my movie based on my memoir was still in the works.

One early afternoon in October 2018, I was out shopping and in a dressing room trying on clothes, when I received a call from one of the documentary producers. I was assuring him he didn't catch me at a bad time. He was informing me that the trailer for the documentary was just released, and he wanted to give me a heads up because I was in the trailer. My heart sunk and that feeling of being judged and ridiculed came over me, again. I swear I wouldn't wish these feelings on my worse enemy. He also said they were

pushing for the documentary to release before
Thanksgiving. I thanked him for letting me know and I
hung up. I started having this anxiety attack and sat on
the small bench in the dressing room. I logged into my
email and pressed play on the trailer and tears fell .

The 2 minute trailer included clips of me in the cage
with Rob on tour, me crying , two other women
breaking down and people picketing outside his shows.
This dramatic music was playing in the background of
the trailer and it gave me chills. I called another
woman who was involved in the documentary and we
were both in tears, it was real now. After months of me
wrapping my part, and later hearing that it may or may
not release due to certain difficulties behind the scenes,
the trailer was officially out for media to repost, and
blogs immediately began putting it up. The feeling of
relief hit me. As I looked around, I realized, I was still
in the fucking dressing room (I laughed at myself) and
got the hell out of there. I walked fast to my car after

purchasing some clothing, and sat looking for news outlets on my phone that posted the trailer, wondering what they thought. So far it seemed everyone was touched by the trailer, but as soon as I reluctantly went onto two urban blogs who posted it, the comments were disgusting, and it was the last time I gave them the time of day. I emailed one popular urban blog and asked them to never post me again because I didn't think the intent was genuine, and that their audience was too ignorant for the content. The bloggers reply didn't appreciate me asking her to remove me but she took it down .

Ignorance had continued to rub me the wrong way. The urban blog owned by a black woman, went on to post a photo of another victim from another case, I was numb reading the comments. (screenshots from blog comment section included in this chapter)

In addition to urban blog negativity, someone else who had come forward informed me that certain others (not the production staff or anyone at Lifetime) involved with the documentary were pissed that I was highlighted in the trailer and they weren't. I got a full story on how they didn't think I deserved to be apart of the documentary because I wasn't underage. What was also mind blowing, they started rumors that Lifetime was trying to promote me heavily because they had my book rights for a film, this was the most ridiculous shit I ever heard. My film and the documentary were separate business and one came before the other. I couldn't start playing myself down and take a back seat to comfort other people. I lived through that hell with Rob and the current media bullshit too, how dare them! Even if they were promoting me why is this a problem if our common goal is to highlight what Rob had continued to do to women and young girls? This was not about who was getting attention or not, but some saw things differently. I had no idea this was becoming some disgusting competition and the goal was to paint me as being after money to the public so no one would support me. Fake accounts were being made and trolls started attacking me again, I knew who it was. They also went to YouTube bloggers in hopes to help spread vicious rumors about me, saying that I never went to police about being abused (my statue of limitations had ran out to file charges, but the ignorance, and jealousy was too strong for them to care that I had addressed this a million times already) and they said I hired a lawyer just for entertainment instead of a criminal lawyer (the same lawyer from the beginning was there to help me release statements and look over contracts and offers that had come my way) .

The strongest person in the world would have thrown in the towel by then and I almost did. I was in disbelief, but I wasn't about to give them the satisfaction. I had a purpose in this too and any blessings that had landed in my lap was well deserved. Anyone truly familiar with my story knew everything that I'd lost with R.Kelly including a thriving career. There was also a text going around saying that I better not be the face of the documentary when my PSA had aired a few months prior. I was floored that this was happening behind my back and I didn't understand the psyche of these people. I got that they wanted to be heard too, but why harass me, and attempt to destroy my character because your shit isn't turning out the way you hoped? My temper was flaring thinking; Bitch I'm not the enemy here! Redirect your fucking anger towards the man who hurt you or your family not me! I tried hard to not respond online or publicly to this. I was asked to do a lot of press and media because I had good representation and had plenty to share about my time with Rob, and most importantly I was credible. I also carried myself with dignity and class. Many media people I had encounters with were impressed with my background and enjoyed speaking with me. Being attacked and sabotaged by people who had come forward against Rob was the most disgusting and foul shit I experienced in this journey next to the urban blogs. These people didn't know me, and had only seen me in articles like the rest of the world. This group of people hated my guts and my whole journey. I hadn't done a thing to them. I wasn't into cliques, complaining that someone else was getting publicity, or talking on the phone about Rob all day. I may not have been underage when I met him but I was credible and the right people believed me. I figured they only wanted one side of him highlighted and my story wasn't about pedophilia. Again, there are many layers to Robert Kelly and I had a right to speak on my time with him, no matter who it rubbed the wrong way.

I had come a long way in my personal life and in this journey. After processing all this sick and vile bullshit I made a vow to stay to myself, as I had been, and to ignore it all. I didn't see Harvey Weinstein or Bill Cosby's accusers being posted by blogs or trolled to death or even going after each other. I was always told by my mom, to keep my hands clean, and when people are digging holes for you, they end up falling into the hole themselves. Bingo ! Mom was right, this happened in later months to come. Karma is a major bitch, and I loved her!

This personal behind the scenes attack on me was messy and I was gearing up to fight back through my lawyer after finding out a long list of things they were doing to sabotage me. After people closest to me talked me out of it, I agreed to drop my intentions so that it would not distract the public, and media from the true purpose.

Despite all these disturbing tactics, there was still a lot of good in my life and the support outweighed anything negative. I still had reasons to hold my head high and I knew with each new level I would face new demons.

November came and they pushed back the release date to January I was a little saddened by this. I had gotten worked up to finally have this out so some unanswered questions could be put to rest. Lifetime network set up a screening for us all to attend in December. I wasn't excited about the screening because I wasn't comfortable watching this in front of people I didn't know. I also didn't care for the sabotage I had experienced, and didn't care to see or meet some of the people behind it all. The screening was shut down within minutes of us watching it in a room full of reporters and media people. My attorney had flown in to accompany me at this screening and we were sitting front row. The screening started after the lights dimmed and moments later they came back on. I saw a few executives appearing a bit worried and I didn't know why. They announced that we had to evacuate the building and that two gun threats were called in.

I was frightened, shocked, and then confused, but felt certain where it came from. Someone was trying to silence us again and it did nothing but ignite fire in me. I knew instantly that something big would come out, when the documentary debuted on tv.

Note: I had no idea that they decided to name the doc: Surviving R.Kelly (the same as my Rolling Stone article) until the trailer had come out. I didn't own the rights to that title. But several people associated with the documentary made accusations that this was promoting me which was false, more defamation.

During this time, I received several concerned calls, and emails of people worried about me, because the gun threat had traveled through news and social media quickly. This gun threat made the public more curious about what the hell was in the documentary, and why they wanted to make sure it wasn't viewed ? Millions became anxious to watch "Surviving R.Kelly".

Chapter Eight:
Surviving Everybody

~ Disappointments are not meant to destroy , they are meant to strengthen us and give us fortitude to accomplish our God given destiny.~

I began deep meditation and using breathing practices, our breath is a powerful tool to ease stress and make you feel less anxious. My self-care was becoming top priority. I was catering to the masses and giving my thoughts it seemed everyday at one point. I started creating boundaries in these interviews letting these people know that I wasn't going to walk through certain topics anymore. I had already addressed the salaciousness and was done, they could very well go back and see what I previously said. I was starting to take a backseat leading up to the last few weeks before the documentary aired. Holidays were here and I wanted to take it all in with a prayer and have a peace of mind.

I loved feeling like a powerful woman, it felt great overcoming all that I had. Many people see the end results of things and are quick to put together your life through photos that you share online, they have no idea what secret hell you may be living or surviving. This journey definitely matured me in many areas.

Most who supported my memoir " I Was Somebody Before This" continued to follow my journey. I had thousands of social media followers and I was updating everyone on the happenings with the documentary and film as well as posting the PSA. I started volunteering around the holidays at shelters and lining up speaking engagements. I wanted to do something to help empower those who didn't see light outside of the darkness they were in. I didn't want to always talk about my ex but I knew it was the reason I ended up in this position to inspire.

I didn't know the nights that I was crying myself to sleep, wanting my life to end, that it was preparing me for these moments. I was close to giving up on my faith several times because I didn't know why certain things were happening to me. I wasn't sure how these life lessons would be positive. Each time things ended up in my favor I knew it had to be because I was doing the right thing and keeping my hands clean. Finding your life's purpose is stressful, many of us think we should automatically know what it is. I had clues along the way and it kept circling back to me using my voice. Who knew that I would go from a little girl seeing her mom be abused to later becoming an active volunteer at battered women's shelters and an advocate. Doing the domestic violence PSA was such an honor and one of the greatest things I've done publicly.

I loved discovering my purpose. In my heart of hearts, I deeply missed radio. There were moments that I would get offers in the last year but I knew I wouldn't have the time to dedicate. Working in radio was always my favorite outlet in my past when things got rough. Music is a mood changer, and it can be both healing and an escape from the world. I enjoyed bringing a smile to my listening audience during my time in radio. My desire to return was still in my heart, but in due time.

One night I prayed about my true purpose and then it hit me that I was living it and that it was about to get even bigger than I could ever imagine. Writing my memoir was about my truth being here, long after I'm gone. Sharing my experiences and how I survived my toughest and most humiliating times has been liberating. It feels like I was given this assignment, this was bigger than just me. People magazine was calling to set up a photo shoot so we could be the first issue going into 2019. I heard that many media people had already previewed the documentary privately before it aired and some were tweeting about how it affected them. Days away from its debut, I knew that my new

year was going to be all about my purpose, I had come
a long way and I accepted that.

Chapter Nine:
Attached Forever

~My truth will live in the pages of my books long after I'm gone, my words will live forever~Kitti Jones

I yearned for my life to be normal again. It seemed that every time I'd have weeks of normalcy, like clockwork, something else scandalous would occur and interviews would be requested again of my thoughts or experiences. Family and friends were great distractions and I loved having days and moments that none of the stuff in the media would enter my mind . Social media became my worse nightmare because it was constant bullshit. I would see people (including famous) who I had great admiration or respect for post support for R.Kelly, post memes for laughs, and say the dumbest shit like there was this huge conspiracy to take down black men. Bill Cosby had been held accountable for his crimes and many in the black community started to look at the documentary as this huge shake down that all the accusers were apart of, I was offended and pissed. One singer I had words with on my twitter account had some comments about how many women would be waiting for R.Kelly backstage and how she witnessed it, in other words she was building up a narrative like we were asking for "it". None of what she said made sense, or could excuse him being abusive to me or taking advantage of underage girls! How stupid! I ultimately ended up blocking her. I personally didn't pursue him or expect that he would beat and starve me. This particular woman was someone he had known since the 90s and had a very popular song with her in the early 2000s. During my time with Rob he mentioned that he had been with her romantically so I knew when I saw her defend him, where it stemmed from. Ironically she had recently spoken publicly about being raped as a young girl, so it hurt to see her have no regards to our stories, it was sick and disappointing. Many women who had secret abusive pasts were ironically being the most vicious towards other others coming forward, it's twisted as fuck. Projecting?

All these men and women were still dead set on turning a blind eye "pre-documentary" although my story and others had been circulating with evidence for over a year. They didn't give a fuck, they viewed us as "clout chasing" (in the black community this was a new overused term to accuse someone of wanting fame by attaching themselves to someone popular. I hated having to constantly remind people that I did not come forward for fame or money. I never gave a damn about being well known. It's certainly not glamorous to be known for being beaten, starved, and being involved in humiliating sex acts. As for money, it was never my motivation. I never got paid once for an interview. I've made money due to my hard work I put into my book and other businesses.

My heart was pure in this and I was not driven by fame, notoriety, or wealth. God knew my intentions and this is why so many great opportunities were coming to me. I didn't seek out people, it was the other way around.

When you know what your purpose is you're not afraid and you know what you need to do.

God gives you grace when you know your place .

I had grown tired of giving interviews, it was the first week of January 2019 and a few days away from the air date of " Surviving R.Kelly". The interviewers were fixated on how old I was when I met him, which I found offensive because my story was never about underage sex or pedophilia. I wanted them to respect that I was even talking to them about such horrifying things, and to not badger me about "Why a grown woman ......". I was seeing a grown man that I was attracted to and I didn't take his past seriously at the time that's why!!! I figured they were out to make me feel shame, like, what was the fucking point? It happened already, I survived it and I'm brave enough to tell. It had been a little over a year that my name had been circulating and I knew that some of these journalists were asking me certain questions to rattle me. I started declining interviews again or just saying I was not talking about that or flat out ignoring them.

More trailers were released and I recorded a radio promo for the documentary as well. On January 5th, 2019 I didn't eat, this was the night Surviving R.Kelly would be viewed by millions. This was a much different feeling from an article being released because most people are visual and don't like to take a lot of time to read. The world would be watching me and other people who had similar stories describe in graphic detail our moments of darkness. I was scared, this was bigger than I initially believed and I avoided family and friends requests to view it with me. The only person I was comfortable with was my son on night one, he wanted to sit in the living area with me and watch as support. I don't think anyone became offended except one associate that kept texting me and asking why wasn't I returning her text, and eventually became unhinged sending me a long paragraph about how I don't respond anymore. The insensitivity from this associate of what I was feeling and not giving me space was disgusting. I knew it was more about her trying to assess my feelings and thoughts before the airing and I didn't like it. I also felt weird about people asking to gather at my house as sort of a watch party and I didn't see it as entertaining, this was a man I could barely look at, my abuser. No way was I going to be celebrating this night like it was a super bowl, I wanted to be alone. If I felt like crying or turning it off I could do that in the privacy of my home with no company to send home.

In the last hour before it aired I text my attorney, two members of my family, a producer from the documentary and a survivor. Lifetime sent emails

ahead of the airing with a list of crisis lines to call if
we needed counselors, whom were standing by to
speak with us, if we needed professional help after
viewing. The show came in with a disclaimer and
warning, my heart was pumping fast. There was a
timeline of how his life started as a child and how he
was abused and much more. My heart ached for Rob
because I remembered him personally sharing these
stories with me when we were together. My son was
annoyed because he felt that it was making people feel
bad for him, and dismissive towards his victims or
survivors. I had to explain to him that there are people
hearing about Rob for the first time and this
background information will help them piece this
altogether. I was not sure how the public was receiving
this so far and was afraid to look at social media.
Many people get general public and social media
opinions confused. I was able to sit through night one
but sadness took over me.

My phone messages were coming by the dozens and I was afraid to read it. I opened my text and saw how many people were saying they cried and realized this was really affecting people while watching. I opened my social media and the documentary was trending number one worldwide!!!! What!!! I quickly became anxious to see if social media was supportive of the first night and it was an overwhelming amount of

people blown away and admitting they had been
ignorant all these years when hearing about him.
Several big name celebrities began tweeting about
silencing R.Kelly and how black girls mattered and the
hashtag #survivingrkelly was number one that night
leading into the next morning.
When people went back to their jobs after night one,
they were all discussing the documentary, morning
radio shows were promoting night two, and this
brought even more millions curious to tune in.

I shut down, I didn't want to interview with anyone to
discuss night one or leave my home. I was only
speaking with the same few people in my circle and
just trying to decompress. Nights two and three fell on
a Friday and Saturday. I was stoic watching myself
relive those details, it was traumatic and triggering. I
wasn't exactly happy with the way my story was
presented, because unlike Rolling Stone, the
documentary edited me heavily. There was a flashback
to our tour skit of Rob handing me contract which was

just a prop for the tour show, they took out the story of us having lunch one afternoon and Rob suggesting I sign this fake confession as collateral in case I ever left him (which he never ended up giving me). In the documentary, it went from me grabbing this prop contract, to me saying "he asked me sign this contract when we got home" making it appear it was the same day and same contract/fake confession.

The part that really annoyed me was how they edited the day I decided to leave Rob. I explained this several times publicly, but in the documentary, it was edited to seem as if I told him I just wanted to go home, and he bought me a ticket (like ok bye) and I called him to go back once at the airport, and he wouldn't answer the phone. Very wrong, it skipped the part about me telling him I wanted to take my son shopping as an excuse to leave town, it skipped that I had a round trip ticket, and Rob had no idea I wasn't planning to return. It also skipped that once at the airport, I became scared about my plan to leave for good, and called him in hopes of hearing his voice to change my mind to go back. I hated being back in a position to fill all these holes again because of this. I was happy for the network and the people who put the work into it, but it wasn't exactly a happy occasion for me. I felt that the documentary did justice shedding light on what was happening and it definitely became a heavy conversation starter. Many high profile people began supporting us and cutting ties with Robert. I hated being put back in a defensive position, because my part left many confused. It wasn't over for me, I stopped bitching about it, and began doing something about it. There's nothing more frustrating than trusting others to tell your story and they fail you. Being an author has freed me. The hardest obstacles are the very ones that end up teaching us the best lesson.

There was a massive amount of support, my inbox was filled with support, and the sales of my memoir was skyrocketing beyond what I had ever seen! Although the editing upset me, my story still resonated with millions. Women and young girls were emailing me, thanking me for sharing my story. Many connected with my pain. These messages made me feel better. I tried to put my disappointments it in the back of my mind. I just wanted some peace. But wait, I thought, hold on, no sweat, my film will be there to fill those holes and answer those questions and clean up the editing that happened to me. What a relief to know my voice wouldn't feel silenced again, or would it?

Sunday was difficult, the documentary was still the talk of social media and offline. I didn't want to leave my house but my childhood friends insisted I step out for a fun late night to grab ice cream, they knew my favorite things to do. I had mixed feelings about everything and they could tell. Some of the trolling was strong supporting R.Kelly there was a page created to post negative things mainly the survivors who appeared on the show, it was vicious, attacking looks, hair wigs, alleged criminal backgrounds, and old videos allegedly exposing contradiction of a few participants. Once I realized the bullying had started again, it motivated me to post more positive comments and screenshots of hundreds of supporters. I had come too far to back down and let these assholes get under my skin. I was tired of letting this entire story control me or how I felt from day to day.

I woke up the next day and decided to re-enter therapy for the second time since coming forward. I wasn't feeling wacky, I just wanted to make sense of everything and my self care started to be number one. I used the same therapist from the year before and I left feeling refreshed. I couldn't get a phrase out of my mind "We heal as we reveal " how compelling, I thought. We have to allow ourselves to confront past hurts, it's the most healing and rewarding thing you can do for yourself.

I started to realize no matter how disappointed I was in the documentary's editing process, those who wanted to seek my truth will find it. I'd already made it available through my book and those who refuse to seek my truth will live in their ignorance forever. I was at peace. I let go of all the hurts from my past, all the bitterness I felt towards anyone, including urban bloggers who use their platforms for bullying and taunting. I was over the people who tried to ruin my name and the ones who attempted to silence me. It was liberating taking back my power, my voice, my dignity and my reputation. I stood for something amazing, I stood with survivors across the world! I will forever be attached to the documentary, articles, and interviews, and I was not ashamed of any of it.

I couldn't help but wonder where I'd be now if I'd never opened that message in my inbox. Would I still be in Kansas? God has his way of making you uncomfortable when it's time for you to walk into your purpose. It all made perfect sense. A beautiful life was waiting for me, and I was ready to finally step into it unapologetically.

Bonus:
Chapter Ten:
Supporters Dedication

My heart will forever be filled with gratitude from all the support and thousands of messages over the past two years. Thank you all from the bottom of my soul. Thank you Rolling Stone, Jason Newman, Spin Magazine, The Root, The Lily, People, New York Times, and Dallas Observer. Thank you all for your responsible and professional journalism. 🩶

The Women I'm Thankful For

Nelson, Diana Nyad, Rose McGowan and Ashley Judd, Lupita Nyong'o and Annabella Sciorra, Kitti Jones, the latest to make allegations against R. Kelly. And, of course, Anita Hill, who endured such scorn and shame, who cracked open the basement door and let the first beams of light shine through.

View Insights

♥ ○ ▽

Promote

⌗

today and it is a Must read. Written by one of the women RKelly abused over the years - @ikittijones . Here are my thoughts/feelings about it: 1) Good for Kitti for taking control of HER story and experience by writing a book. Instead of relying on interviewers to do so, subject to editing, opinions, etc. Anyone who views that as some kind of twisted 'opportunity' is ignorant as she continues to take a lot of ridicule that I don't think I would be strong enough to endure. Her story and the others are helping a lot of people and has prompted me to do some self reflection. 2) People wonder 'well why did they stay and take it?' 'Why didn't they just leave?'

😌 😆 ♥ 😍 😇 😡 😊 😊

Wednesday 9:43 AM

with you! Encouraged by your strength. In addition... Great book! I bought on Amazon...and can't wait for your next book! Blessings to you and continued healing! 💕 💜 💕

I'm soooo proud of you for coming forward! Most women do not have that courage. I believe you!!!

💜 🌙

Wednesday 6:41 AM

Your such a beautiful soul and strong woman 💜 💜 💜 💜 don't let no one tell u different

💜 🌙

8:53 PM

Thank you for sharing your story in the docu-series. Strength! Dignity! Power! Woman! I cant begin to imagine all that you tell in your book. Im ready to read! God Bless You! 🙏

💜 🌙

7:19 PM

5:52 PM

You are unreal, you're so strong and absolutely beautiful. I'm not a creep I swear 😅 I was just blown away by how strong and courageous you are. If you are ever in London U.K it would be an honour to meet up and take you out

Kitti Jones went on to speak at : Real Screen Summit, Deadline Contenders, Emmy FYC in New York, Variety's Women of Power Luncheon, Banff Media Festival in Canada, and at campuses and women's shelters. Kitti has also been offered a new radio position at a radio station in the Los Angeles area.

The film based on her memoir "I Was Somebody Before This" is still in development after being nixed then picked back up.

Robert Kelly was later indicted on multiple sexual abuse charges, and was being investigated by the FBI for alleged sex trafficking following the airing of the documentary.

For bookings or speaking engagements go to:
www.kittijonesonline.com

CPSIA information can be obtained
at www.ICGtesting.com
Printed in the USA
LVHW091829171019
634537LV00006B/928/P